meatballs

meatballs

30 recipes for mouth watering variations

First published in 2011
LOVE FOOD is an imprint of Parragon Books Ltd

Parragon
Queen Street House
4 Queen Street
Bath BA1 1HE, UK

ISBN: 978-1-4454-2874-1

Printed in China

Introduction written by Christine France
Additional recipes written by Christine France
Cover and additional internal photography by Clive Bozzard-Hill
Home economy and food styling by Valerie Barratt

Notes for the Reader
This book uses both metric and imperial measurements. Follow the same
units of measurement throughout; do not mix metric and imperial. All spoon
measurements are level: teaspoons are assumed to be 5 ml, and tablespoons are
assumed to be 15 ml. Unless otherwise stated, milk is assumed to be full fat, eggs
and individual vegetables are medium, and pepper is freshly ground black pepper.

The times given are an approximate guide only. Preparation times differ according
to the techniques used by different people and the cooking times may also vary
from those given. Optional ingredients, variations or serving suggestions have not
been included in the calculations.

Recipes using raw or very lightly cooked eggs should be avoided by infants, the
elderly, pregnant women, convalescents and anyone suffering from an illness.
Pregnant and breastfeeding women are advised to avoid eating peanuts and
peanut products. Sufferers from nut allergies should be aware that some of the
ready-made ingredients used in the recipes in this book may contain nuts. Always
check the packaging before use.

Contents

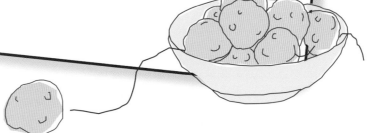

What is a meatball?

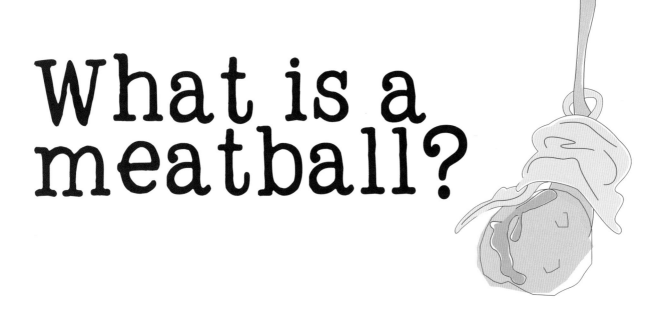

A meatball can be just about anything that can be ground and ends up round! Meatballs are not just for spaghetti, so be adventurous and try them in other ways, too.

Almost every nation has its own variation on the meatball theme, many making use of different meats and flavour additions such as herbs and spices, from spicy Middle Eastern koftas to the more delicate Northern European frikadeller (flat, pan-fried dumplings of ground meat).

Perhaps the reason meatballs are so popular is that they are economical and very easy to make. They're also endlessly versatile, and can be the base for quick, nourishing family suppers or party dishes, soups, packed lunches, sandwiches or canapés.

Meatballs can be fried, grilled, braised, poached, steamed, baked or microwaved.

Which meat to choose?

Meatballs can be made with any good-quality meat that can be minced: beef, pork, ham, bacon, lamb, turkey, chicken or game.

When shopping for meat to use for meatballs, remember that it's not always the very expensive cuts such as beef fillet, pork tenderloin or chicken breasts, that are best because they can be very low in fat. Instead, choose one of the cheaper cuts that tend to have slightly more fat to help make more moist, flavourful meatballs.

When buying ready-made minced meats, don't be tempted to buy the cheapest mince on the counter as this can be very high in fat, which will not only make your meatballs too greasy but much of the fat will cook out and the meatballs will shrink.

Some meats, such as chicken, are not widely available in minced form. If you don't have a mincer at home, a food processor can do the job. Use the 'pulse' button to avoid over-processing, because it's important to retain some texture and not reduce the meat to mush. In the case of chicken, the thigh meat is the best choice for tasty, moist meatballs.

Not just meat

Seafood, including fish fillets or even shellfish, can be made into tasty fish balls, too. Even vegetarians needn't miss out, as all kinds of vegetables and pulses can be used as a base for veggie balls.

Texture enhancers

Bread or breadcrumbs, either white or wholemeal, are often added to meatballs as a binder and they also create a softer consistency. The bread can be soaked in water or milk first, but take care not to add too much liquid or the meatballs will be too soft.

Other grains, such as rice, oatmeal, cornmeal, or cracker crumbs can be used in the same way as bread and are a useful extender for the meat when you're on a budget.

Seeds or nuts add a delicious crunch to simple meatballs, either added to the mix or used as a coating.

Moisture givers

The amount of moisture needed in meatballs depends on the cooking method. For threading on to skewers or for frying, keep the mixture fairly firm, as soft, wet mixtures will lose their shape or fall apart. More moist mixtures are best cooked in a sauce or baked in the oven.

Some meatball mixtures are bound with beaten egg to keep the ingredients firmly together, or simply enriched with egg yolk. Grated cheese, or finely chopped vegetables – onions being the most popular – will add moisture as well as pepping up the colour, texture and flavour. Try raw grated carrots, courgettes or beetroot for a change.

Flavour boosters

Meatballs can be spiced up with almost anything that takes your fancy. If you like spicy food, try adding crushed chillies or chilli sauce, or for a more subtle, warm spice use a little curry powder or paste, or cumin, coriander or cinnamon.

Herbs are the perfect flavour addition to meatballs, either fresh or dried. The most useful to keep in your storecupboard are parsley, thyme, coriander, chives and rosemary.

A dash of Worcestershire sauce, ketchup or mustard can add a zip to a plain meatball mix in seconds.

And don't forget the salt and freshly ground pepper – if you're not sure how much to add, fry a small amount of the mixture in a little oil so you can taste to check the seasoning, before cooking the rest.

Top tips

- Choose good-quality mince with not too much fat.

- Make sure all your meatballs are the same size, so they cook evenly.

- Use a small ice-cream scoop to portion out the mixture for rolling into balls. Tiny ones can be scooped with a melon baller.

- For most purposes, the perfect size of meatball is about 4–5 cm/1½–2 inches in diameter; larger ones are difficult to cook evenly unless in a sauce. Meatballs for canapés are usually smaller, bite-sized mouthfuls.

- Your hands are the best tool for shaping meatballs. Roll the mixture between your palms to get a firm, round shape every time.

- Lightly wet your hands when shaping to prevent soft mixtures from sticking.

- If the meatballs are to be shallow fried, coat lightly in flour or fine breadcrumbs to form a crust on the outside.

- When time allows, it helps to chill the meatballs for at least 10 minutes before cooking, to allow the texture to firm up slightly and for the flavours to combine.

- A wok makes a good cooking pot for frying meatballs as they can be moved around easily without breaking up.

- Use a couple of palette knives or spatulas instead of tongs to turn the meatballs when cooking to prevent the mixture breaking up.

- Drain off any excess fat from fried meatballs by placing onto kitchen paper before adding to sauces or serving plain.

Freezing

Meatballs are perfect for freezing, so if you're making a batch of meatballs, it's worth making double the quantity to keep for another day.

Shape the meatballs as usual and open-freeze on a baking sheet, or cook first then cool completely before freezing. When frozen solid, the meatballs can be transferred into sealed polythene bags or freezer boxes for storage.

Most types of meatball can be frozen successfully for 3–4 months, but if the recipe contains garlic, freeze for only 1 month before use.

To use, thaw overnight in the refrigerator before cooking or reheating. To cook from frozen, allow extra cooking time and test to make sure the meatballs are thoroughly cooked.

Avoid cooking raw poultry from frozen. Allow meats such as chicken and turkey to thaw out completely, before cooking.

Saucy

spaghetti & meatballs

serves 4

1 tbsp olive oil

1 small onion, finely chopped

2 garlic cloves, finely chopped

2 fresh thyme sprigs, finely chopped

650 g/1 lb 7 oz fresh beef mince

25 g/1 oz fresh breadcrumbs

1 egg, lightly beaten

450 g/1 lb dried spaghetti

salt and pepper

sauce

1 onion, cut into wedges

3 red peppers, halved and deseeded

400 g/14 oz canned chopped tomatoes

1 bay leaf

salt and pepper

Heat the oil in a frying pan. Add the chopped onion and garlic and cook over a low heat, for 5 minutes, until softened. Remove from the heat and place into a bowl with the thyme, minced beef, breadcrumbs and egg. Season to taste and mix thoroughly. Shape the mixture into 20 equal-sized balls.

Heat a large non-stick frying pan over a low–medium heat. Add the meatballs and cook, stirring gently and turning frequently, for 15 minutes, until lightly browned all over.

Meanwhile for the sauce, preheat the grill. Put the onion wedges and pepper halves, skin-side up, on a grill rack and cook under the preheated grill, turning frequently, for 10 minutes, until the pepper skins are blistered and charred. Put the peppers into a plastic bag, tie the top and leave to cool. Set the onion wedges aside.

Peel off the pepper skins. Roughly chop the flesh and put it into a food processor or blender with the onion wedges and tomatoes. Process to a smooth purée and season to taste with salt and pepper. Pour into a saucepan with the bay leaf and bring to the boil. Reduce the heat and simmer, stirring occasionally, for 10 minutes. Remove and discard the bay leaf.

Meanwhile, bring a saucepan of salted water to the boil. Add the spaghetti, return to the boil and cook for 8–10 minutes, or according to the package directions, until tender but still firm to the bite. Drain the spaghetti and serve immediately with the meatballs and sauce.

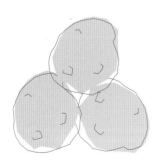

meatballs in almond sauce

serves 6-8

55 g/2 oz white bread, crusts removed

3 tbsp water

450 g/1 lb fresh pork mince

1 large onion, chopped

1 garlic clove, crushed

2 tbsp fresh parsley, chopped, plus extra to garnish

1 egg, beaten

freshly grated nutmeg

plain flour, for coating

2 tbsp Spanish olive oil

lemon juice, to taste

salt and pepper

almond sauce

2 tbsp Spanish olive oil

25 g/1 oz white bread

115 g/4 oz blanched almonds

2 garlic cloves, chopped

150 ml/5 fl oz dry white wine

425 ml/15 fl oz vegetable stock

salt and pepper

Place the bread into a bowl, add the water and leave to soak for 5 minutes. Squeeze out the water and place into a bowl with the minced pork, onion, garlic, parsley and egg. Season to taste with nutmeg and salt and pepper and mix thoroughly.

Dust your hands lightly with flour and shape the mixture into 30 equal-sized balls. Lightly dust each meatball with flour. Heat the olive oil in a large, heavy-based frying pan. Add the meatballs, in batches, and fry for 4–5 minutes, or until browned on all sides. Using a slotted spoon, remove the meatballs from the pan and reserve.

To make the sauce, heat the olive oil in the same frying pan in which the meatballs were fried. Break the bread into pieces, add to the pan with the almonds and fry gently, stirring, until the bread and almonds are golden brown. Add the garlic and fry for a further 30 seconds, then pour in the wine and boil for 1–2 minutes. Season to taste with salt and pepper and leave to cool slightly. Transfer to a food processor or blender. Pour in the vegetable stock and process the mixture until smooth. Return the sauce to the frying pan.

Carefully add the meatballs to the almond sauce and simmer for 25 minutes, or until the meatballs are tender. Taste the sauce and season with salt and pepper if necessary. Transfer to a warmed serving dish, then add a squeeze of lemon juice to taste and sprinkle with chopped parsley. Serve immediately.

meatballs with cracked olives

serves 6

55 g/2 oz day-old bread, crusts removed

3 tbsp water

250 g/9 oz lean fresh pork mince

250 g/9 oz lean fresh lamb mince

2 small onions, finely chopped

3 garlic cloves, crushed

1 tsp ground cumin

1 tsp ground coriander

1 egg, lightly beaten

plain flour, for dusting

3 tbsp Spanish olive oil

400 g/14 oz canned chopped tomatoes

5 tbsp dry sherry or red wine

pinch of hot or sweet smoked Spanish paprika

pinch of sugar

175 g/6 oz cracked green olives in extra virgin olive oil

salt and pepper

crusty bread, to serve

Place the bread into a bowl, add the water and leave to soak for 30 minutes. Squeeze out as much of the water as possible and place into a dry bowl with the pork and lamb mince, 1 chopped onion, 2 crushed garlic cloves, the cumin, coriander and egg. Season to taste with salt and pepper and mix thoroughly. Dust your hands lightly with flour and shape the mixture into equal-sized balls. Lightly dust each meatball with flour.

Heat 2 tablespoons of the oil in a large frying pan, add the meatballs, in batches to avoid overcrowding, and cook over a medium heat, turning frequently, for 8–10 minutes until golden brown on all sides and firm. Remove with a slotted spoon and set aside.

Heat the remaining oil in the frying pan, add the remaining onion and cook, stirring occasionally, for 5 minutes, or until softened but not browned. Add the remaining garlic and cook, stirring, for 30 seconds. Add the tomatoes and their juice, sherry, paprika and sugar and season to taste with salt. Bring to the boil, then reduce the heat and simmer for 10 minutes.

Using a hand-held blender, blend the tomato mixture until smooth. Alternatively, turn the tomato mixture into a food processor or blender and process until smooth. Return the sauce to the saucepan.

Carefully return the meatballs to the frying pan and add the olives. Simmer gently for 20 minutes, or until the meatballs are tender. Serve hot, with crusty bread to mop up the sauce.

swedish meatballs

serves 4

2 potatoes, cut into chunks

25 g/1 oz fresh breadcrumbs

650 g/1 lb 7 oz fresh beef mince

1 small onion, grated

1 egg, lightly beaten

1 tsp brown sugar

pinch each of grated nutmeg, ground allspice, ground ginger and ground cloves

55 g/2 oz fine dry breadcrumbs

85 g/3 oz butter

salt and pepper

sauce

2 tbsp plain flour

225 ml/8 fl oz beef stock

225 ml/8 fl oz double cream

salt and pepper

Cook the potatoes in a saucepan of salted boiling water for 20–25 minutes, until tender but not falling apart. Drain, tip into a bowl, mash well and leave to cool slightly.

Add the breadcrumbs, minced beef, onion, egg, sugar and spices to the bowl. Season to taste and mix thoroughly. Shape the mixture into equal-sized balls. Roll the meatballs in the dry breadcrumbs until thoroughly coated.

Melt the butter in a large frying pan. Add the meatballs, in batches, and cook over a medium heat, stirring and turning occasionally, for 10 minutes, until golden brown all over and cooked through. Remove with a slotted spoon, drain on kitchen paper and keep warm while you cook the remaining meatballs.

When all the meatballs have been cooked, keep them warm while you make the sauce. Stir the flour into the frying pan and cook, stirring constantly, for 1 minute. Remove the pan from the heat and gradually stir in the stock, then add the cream. Season to taste with salt and pepper, return the pan to a low heat and cook, stirring constantly, until thickened and smooth.

Return the meatballs to the pan and simmer for 10 minutes. Serve immediately.

meatballs in red wine sauce

serves 4

150 g/5½ oz white breadcrumbs

150 ml/5 fl oz milk

12 shallots, chopped

900 g/2 lb fresh beef mince

1 tsp paprika

450 g/1 lb dried tagliatelle

salt and pepper

1 fresh basil sprig, to garnish

red wine sauce

25 g/1 oz butter

8 tbsp olive oil

225 g/8 oz oyster mushrooms

25 g/1 oz wholemeal flour

200 ml/7 fl oz beef stock

150 ml/5 fl oz red wine

4 tomatoes, peeled and chopped

1 tbsp tomato purée

1 tsp brown sugar

1 tbsp finely chopped fresh basil

salt and pepper

Place the breadcrumbs into a bowl, add the milk and leave to soak for 30 minutes.

To make the sauce, heat half the butter and half the oil in a saucepan over a low heat. Slice the mushrooms, add to the pan and cook for 4 minutes. Stir in the flour and cook for 2 minutes. Add the stock and wine and simmer for 15 minutes. Add the tomatoes, tomato purée, sugar and basil. Season to taste with salt and pepper and cook for 30 minutes.

Preheat the oven to 180°C/350°F/Gas Mark 4. Place the shallots, minced beef, paprika and soaked breadcrumbs into a bowl. Season to taste and mix thoroughly. Shape the mixture into 12 equal-sized balls.

Heat the remaining oil and remaining butter in a large frying pan. Add the meatballs and cook until browned. Transfer to a large casserole dish and pour over the sauce. Bake in the preheated oven for 30 minutes.

Bring a large pan of lightly salted water to the boil over a medium heat. Add the pasta and cook for 8–10 minutes, or according to the package directions, until tender but still firm to the bite. Drain and transfer to a serving dish. Remove the casserole from the oven and pour the meatballs and sauce alongside the pasta. Garnish with a basil sprig and serve immediately.

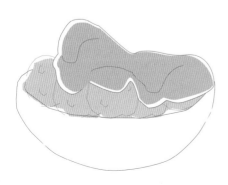

spicy meatball risotto

serves 4

1 thick slice white bread, crusts removed

water or milk, for soaking

450 g/1 lb fresh pork mince

2 garlic cloves, very finely chopped

1 tbsp finely chopped onion

1 tsp black peppercorns, lightly crushed

pinch of salt

1 egg

corn oil, for shallow-frying

400 g/14 oz canned chopped tomatoes

1 tbsp tomato purée

1 tsp dried oregano

1 tsp fennel seeds

pinch of sugar

1 litre/1¾ pints beef stock

1 tbsp olive oil

40 g/1½ oz butter

1 small onion, finely chopped

280 g/10 oz risotto rice

150 ml/5 fl oz red wine

salt and pepper

fresh basil leaves, to garnish

Place the bread into a bowl, add the water and leave to soak for 5 minutes. Squeeze out the water and place into a dry bowl together with the minced pork, garlic, onion, crushed peppercorns and salt. Add the egg and mix thoroughly. Shape the mixture into 12 equal-sized balls.

Heat the corn oil in a frying pan over a medium heat. Add the meatballs and cook through. Remove and drain.

Combine the tomatoes, tomato purée, herbs and sugar in a heavy-based saucepan. Add the meatballs and bring to the boil. Reduce the heat and simmer for 30 minutes.

Bring the stock to a boil in the saucepan, then reduce the heat and keep simmering gently over a low heat while you are cooking the risotto.

Meanwhile, heat the olive oil with 25 g/1 oz of the butter in a deep saucepan until the butter has melted. Stir in the onion and cook for 5 minutes, until golden.

Reduce the heat, add the rice and mix to coat in oil and butter. Cook, stirring constantly, for 2–3 minutes, or until the grains are translucent. Add the wine and cook, stirring constantly until reduced.

Gradually add the simmering stock. Stir constantly and add more liquid as the rice absorbs each addition. Increase the heat so that the liquid bubbles. Cook for 20 minutes. Season to taste.

Lift out the cooked meatballs and add to the risotto. Remove the risotto from the heat and add the remaining butter. Mix well. Arrange the risotto and a few meatballs among 4 plates. Drizzle with the tomato sauce, garnish with the basil and serve.

turkey meatballs with pasta

serves 4

350 g/12 oz fresh turkey mince

1 small garlic clove, finely chopped

2 tbsp finely chopped fresh parsley

1 egg, lightly beaten

plain flour, for dusting

3 tbsp olive oil

1 onion, finely chopped

1 celery stick, finely chopped

1 carrot, finely chopped

400 ml/14 fl oz passata

1 fresh rosemary sprig

1 bay leaf

350 g/12 oz dried penne

salt and pepper

freshly grated Parmesan cheese, to serve

Place the minced turkey, garlic, parsley and egg into a bowl. Season to taste and mix thoroughly. Dust your hands lightly with flour and shape the mixture into equal-sized balls. Lightly dust each meatball with flour.

Heat the oil in a saucepan. Add the onion, celery and carrot and cook over a low heat, stirring occasionally, for 5 minutes, until softened. Increase the heat to medium, add the meatballs and cook, turning frequently, for 8–10 minutes, until golden brown all over.

Pour in the passata, add the rosemary and bay leaf, season to taste with salt and pepper and bring to the boil. Lower the heat, cover and simmer gently, stirring occasionally, for 40–45 minutes. Remove and discard the herbs.

Shortly before the meatballs are ready, bring a large pan of lightly salted water to the boil. Add the pasta, bring back to the boil and cook for 8–10 minutes, or according to the package directions, until tender but still firm to the bite. Drain and add to the pan with the meatballs. Stir gently and heat through briefly, then spoon into individual warmed dishes. Sprinkle generously with Parmesan cheese and serve immediately.

chinese soup with meatballs

serves 4-6

5 dried Chinese mushrooms

350 g/12 oz fresh beef mince

1 onion, finely chopped

1 garlic clove, finely chopped

1 tbsp cornflour

1 egg, lightly beaten

850 ml/1½ pints beef stock

1 bunch of watercress
(about 25 g/1 oz), stalks removed

3 spring onions, finely chopped

1–1½ tbsp soy sauce

Place the mushrooms into a bowl, add warm water to cover and leave to soak for 15 minutes. Squeeze out the water. Discard the stalks and thinly slice the caps.

Place the minced beef, onion, garlic, cornflour and egg into a bowl. Mix thoroughly. Shape the mixture into small equal-sized balls, drop them into a bowl of iced water and leave to stand for 15 minutes.

Pour the stock into a large saucepan and bring to the boil. Drain the meatballs well, add to the pan and bring back to the boil. Reduce the heat and simmer for 10 minutes. Add the mushrooms, watercress, spring onions and soy sauce to taste and simmer for a further 2 minutes. Serve immediately.

Skewered

grecian meatballs

serves 4

450 g/1 lb lean, finely minced lamb

1 medium onion, grated

1 garlic clove, crushed

25 g/1 oz fresh white or brown breadcrumbs

1 tbsp chopped fresh mint

1 tbsp chopped fresh parsley

1 egg, beaten

salt and pepper

olive oil, for brushing

warm pitta and salad, to serve

Place the minced lamb, onion, garlic, breadcrumbs, mint, parsley and egg into a bowl. Season to taste and mix thoroughly. Shape the mixture into 16 small equal-sized balls and thread onto 4 flat metal skewers. Brush the meatballs with oil.

Cook the meatballs under the preheated grill for 10 minutes, turning frequently, and brushing with more oil if necessary, until browned. Serve the meatballs tucked into warm pitta with salad.

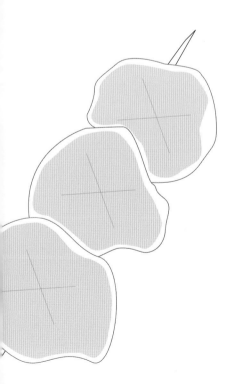

beef & lamb koftas

serves 4

200 g/7 oz fresh beef mince

100 g/3½ oz fresh lamb mince

½ onion, grated

2 tbsp chopped fresh
flat-leaf parsley

1 tbsp chopped fresh coriander

1 garlic clove, very finely chopped

1 tsp ground cumin

¼ tsp ground cinnamon

½ tsp hot paprika, or to taste

½ tsp harissa paste, or to taste

½ tsp salt

pinch of cayenne pepper, or to
taste

olive oil, for brushing

mixed salad and warmed pitta
bread, to serve

Put the beef and lamb mince in a food processor and process to a paste. Add the onion, herbs, garlic, cumin, cinnamon, paprika, harissa paste, salt and cayenne pepper and process again until blended.

Divide the mixture into 4. Wrap the mixture around the skewers to form oval shapes. Cover with clingfilm and chill in the refrigerator for at least 1 hour, but ideally up to 4 hours.

Preheat the grill. Brush the meatballs with a little oil and cook under the preheated grill for 10 minutes, turning frequently, and brushing with more oil if necessary, until cooked through.

Using a folded cloth to protect your fingers, hold the top of each skewer and use a fork to push the meatballs off. Serve with a mixed salad and warmed pitta bread.

lamb koftas & herb salad

serves 4

400 g/14 oz lean minced lamb

1 small onion, finely chopped

2 tsp each ground coriander, ground cumin and paprika

1 tbsp chopped fresh coriander

2 tbsp chopped fresh mint

3 tbsp olive oil

6 tbsp natural yogurt

85 g/3 oz cucumber, grated

2 tsp mint sauce

115 g/4 oz mixed baby leaf and herb salad

1 tbsp lemon juice

salt and pepper

Place 8 wooden skewers in a shallow bowl filled with water and leave to soak for 30 minutes. Place the minced lamb, onion, spices and coriander and mint in a food processor with plenty of salt and pepper. Process for 1–2 minutes until finely minced. Transfer to a bowl and cover and chill in the refrigerator for 30 minutes.

Preheat the grill. Divide the mixture into 8. Wrap the mixture around the soaked wooden skewers to form oval shapes. Brush the meatballs with a little oil and cook under the preheated grill for 15–20 minutes, turning frequently, and brushing with more oil if necessary, until cooked through.

Meanwhile, mix the yogurt, cucumber and mint sauce together in a small bowl and season with salt and pepper.

Place the salad leaves in a large bowl. Whisk together the rest of the oil with the lemon juice and season to taste. Pour the dressing over the salad leaves and toss to coat. Serve the hot koftas with the salad and cucumber-and-mint yogurt.

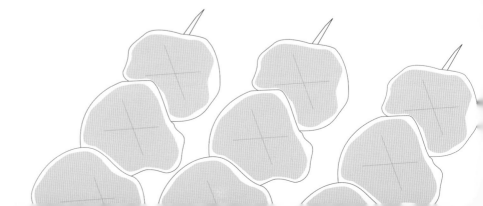

silky chicken kebabs

serves 4-6

55 g/2 oz raw cashew nuts

2 tbsp single cream

1 egg

450 g/1 lb skinless, boneless chicken breasts, roughly chopped

½ tsp salt, or to taste

2 tsp garlic purée

2 tsp ginger purée

2 green chillies, roughly chopped (deseeded if you like)

15 g/½ oz fresh coriander, including the tender stalks, roughly chopped

1 tsp garam masala

25 g/1 oz butter, melted

to serve

mint and spinach chutney

salad greens

Put the cashew nuts in a heatproof bowl, cover with boiling water and leave to soak for 20 minutes. Drain and put in a food processor. Add the cream and egg and process the ingredients to a coarse mixture.

Add all the remaining ingredients, except melted butter, and process until smooth. Transfer to a bowl, cover and chill in the refrigerator for 30 minutes.

Preheat the grill. Divide the mixture into 8. Wrap the mixture around the skewers to form oval shapes. Cook under the preheated grill for 4 minutes, then brush with half the melted butter and cook for a further minute. Turn over and cook for 3 minutes, brush with the remaining melted butter and cook for a further 2 minutes, until cooked through.

Serve with the chutney and salad greens.

meatballs with tomato relish

serves 4

1 onion, finely chopped

2 garlic cloves, finely chopped

2 slices bread, crusts removed

500 g/1 lb 2 oz lean beef, minced

1 cooked baby beetroot, chopped

pinch of paprika

2 tsp finely chopped fresh thyme

1 egg

salt and pepper

fresh thyme sprigs, to garnish

tomato relish

150 ml/5 fl oz passata

2 tsp creamed horseradish

Preheat the oven to 230°C/450°F/Gas Mark 8. To make the tomato relish, mix the passata and creamed horseradish together in a small bowl. Cover and reserve until required.

Place 8 wooden skewers in a shallow bowl filled with cold water and leave to soak for 30 minutes. Place the onion, garlic and 2 teaspoons of water in a small saucepan and simmer over a low heat for 5 minutes. Increase the heat, bring to the boil and cook until all the water has evaporated. Remove from the heat.

Meanwhile, tear the bread into pieces. Place into a bowl, add enough water to cover and leave to soak for 5 minutes. Squeeze out the water and place into a dry bowl with the minced beef, onion-and-garlic mixture, beetroot, paprika, thyme and egg. Season to taste with salt and pepper and mix thoroughly.

Shape the mixture into 24 equal-sized balls, thread onto the soaked wooden skewers and place on a baking sheet. Bake in the preheated oven for 10 minutes, or until cooked through. Transfer to a serving dish, garnish with a few sprigs of fresh thyme and serve with the tomato relish.

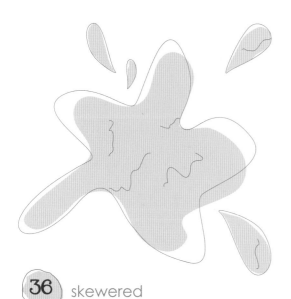

pork & peanut meatballs

serves 6

2 medium red onions

500 g/1 lb 2 oz minced pork

½ tsp dried chilli flakes

85 g/3 oz crunchy peanut butter

40 g/1½ oz fresh white breadcrumbs

finely grated zest of ½ orange

salt and pepper

55 g/2 oz salted peanuts, chopped, to sprinkle

orange salsa

1 orange

1 small red onion, finely diced

1 tbsp olive oil

Soak 6 bamboo skewers in cold water for 10 minutes.

Cut one of the onions into 12 small wedges and set aside. Grate the remaining onion and place in a bowl with the minced pork, chilli, peanut butter, breadcrumbs and orange zest. Season to taste and mix thoroughly. Shape the mixture into 24 small equal-sized balls, thread onto the soaked wooden skewers and place one of the reserved onion wedges at each end.

Place the skewers on a baking sheet, cover and chill for 10 minutes or until required. Preheat the grill.

For the salsa, cut away all the peel and white pith from the orange then separate the segments, catching any juice in a bowl. Roughly chop the segments and add to the bowl with the juice. Then add the diced onion and olive oil to the bowl and mix together thoroughly.

Cook the skewers on the baking sheet under the preheated grill for about 15 minutes, turning occasionally, until golden brown and thoroughly cooked.

Serve the meatballs sprinkled with the chopped peanuts, with the orange salsa on the side.

turkey & rosemary kebabs

serves 4

4 firm twigs of rosemary, about 25 cm/10 inches long

400 g/14 oz minced turkey

80 g/2¾ oz porridge oats

1 medium red pepper, deseeded and finely chopped

1 small onion, very finely chopped

½ tsp smoked paprika

salt and pepper

olive oil, for brushing

Greek yogurt, to serve

fresh salad greens, to serve

Snip the 5 cm/2 inch top sprigs of leaves from the rosemary and reserve 8 sprigs. Strip the remaining leaves from the twigs and soak the sticks in cold water for 10 minutes, then set to one side. Finely chop 1 tablespoon of the rosemary leaves.

Place the turkey, oats, pepper, onion, chopped rosemary leaves and paprika in a bowl. Season to taste and mix thoroughly. Shape into 16 small equal-sized balls and thread onto each rosemary twig.

Place on a lightly greased baking sheet, cover and chill for 10 minutes or until required.

Preheat the grill. Lightly brush the meatballs with oil and cook on the baking sheet under the preheated grill for 15–18 minutes, turning occasionally, and brushing with more oil if necessary, until cooked through.

Press the reserved fresh sprigs of rosemary into one end of each skewer and serve hot with a spoonful of Greek yogurt and fresh salad greens.

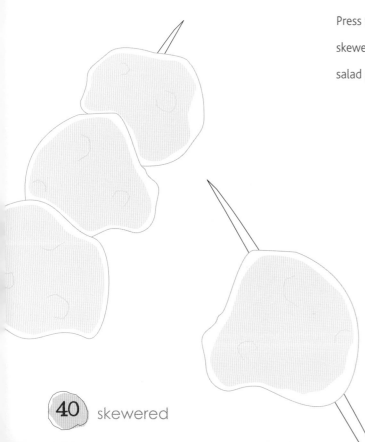

fish & coconut balls

serves 4

groundnut oil, for greasing

3-4 lemon grass stalks

350 g/12 oz monkfish fillet, or other white fish

4 spring onions, chopped

2 tsp Thai green curry paste

100 g/3½ oz peeled prawns, chopped

50 ml/2 fl oz thick coconut milk

55 g/2 oz fresh white breadcrumbs

sesame oil, for brushing

lime wedges, to serve

Preheat the oven to 200°C/400°F/Gas Mark 6. Grease a baking sheet with oil. Cut the lemon grass stalks in quarters lengthways then cut into 9-cm/3½-inch lengths (there should be 12–14 lengths). Soak in cold water for 10 minutes and then set to one side.

Cut the monkfish into chunks and place in a food processor with the spring onions and curry paste. Process for a few seconds until the mixture is fairly finely chopped but still coarse in texture; if the fish is chopped too finely it will become mushy. Put this mixture in a large bowl.

Stir the prawns, coconut milk and breadcrumbs into the bowl with the monkfish mixure and mix thoroughly. Shape the mixture into 12–14 equal-sized balls and place on the prepared baking sheet. Lightly brush the fishballs with sesame oil and press a piece of lemon grass into each ball.

Bake in the preheated oven for 15–20 minutes, until golden brown and just firm. Serve warm with lime wedges as a starter.

Wrapped

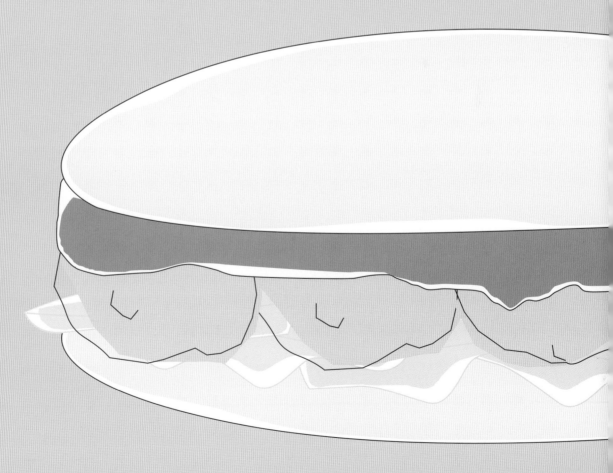

chicken meatballs

serves 4

400 g/14 oz chicken breast, diced

1 eating apple, coarsely grated

50 g/1¾ oz Cheddar cheese, roughly grated

55 g/2 oz fresh white breadcrumbs

2 tbsp chopped chives

salt and pepper

wholemeal flour, for dusting

groundnut oil, for shallow frying

wraps

4 wholemeal wheat tortilla wraps

75g/2¾ watercress or rocket leaves

Place the chicken in a food processor and process on 'pulse' for a few seconds to chop finely. Mix the chicken with the apple, cheese, breadcrumbs, chives, salt and pepper. Shape the mixture into 20 equal-sized balls and roll in flour to coat lightly. Chill for 10 minutes or until required.

Heat a shallow depth of oil in a wok or heavy frying pan and fry the chicken meatballs for 6–8 minutes, turning often, until golden brown and firm. Drain on kitchen paper.

Warm the tortilla wraps slightly, fold over to make pockets and fill with watercress and the meatballs to serve. Wrap with a paper napkin to hold the wrap in place.

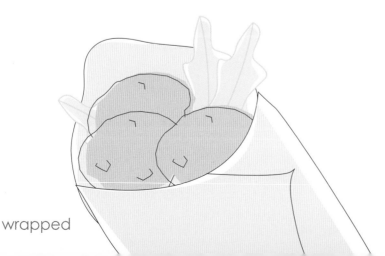

bacon-wrapped turkey meatballs

serves 4

500 g/1 lb 2 oz minced turkey

1 medium onion, very finely chopped

70 g/2½ oz fresh or frozen cranberries, finely chopped

2 tbsp finely chopped sage leaves

salt and pepper

10 slices streaky bacon or pancetta

cranberry sauce, to serve

Place the minced turkey, onion, cranberries and chopped sage into a bowl. Season to taste and mix thoroughly. Shape the mixture into 20 equal-sized balls.

Place the bacon on a chopping board and press each rasher with the back of a knife to stretch thinly.

Cut each rasher in half across the middle and wrap each rasher half around a meatball. Place the meatballs on a baking sheet, cover and chill for 10 minutes or until required.

Preheat the oven to 200°C/400°F/Gas Mark 6. Bake the meatballs on the baking sheet in the preheated oven for 20-25 minutes, or until golden and firm. Serve warm, with the cranberry sauce on the side.

vegetarian aubergine balls

serves 4

2 large aubergines

olive oil, plus extra for brushing

salt and pepper

1 medium red onion

2 cloves garlic, crushed

225 g/8 oz stale white breadcrumbs

85 g/3 oz finely grated Parmesan cheese

2 egg yolks

3 tbsp chopped basil

plain flour, for dusting

4 corn tortilla wraps, warmed, to serve

sprigs of basil, to garnish

salt and pepper

salsa

200 g/7 oz baby plum tomatoes, chopped

2 tsp red wine vinegar

1 tsp light muscovado sugar

1 tbsp capers, rinsed and finely chopped

salt and pepper

Preheat the oven to 200°C/400°F/Gas Mark 6.

Halve the aubergines lengthways, brush with oil, sprinkle with salt and pepper and place, cut-side down, on a baking sheet. Halve the onion, leaving on the skin, and place, cut-side down, on the baking sheet. Roast the aubergines and onion in the preheated oven for 20–25 minutes until tender. Then remove from oven and allow to cool.

Scoop out the flesh from the aubergine and chop. Peel off the onion skin and finely chop the onion. Place the aubergine, onion, garlic, breadcrumbs, Parmesan cheese, egg yolks and basil into a bowl. Season to taste and mix thoroughly. Shape the mixture into 20 equal-sized balls using floured hands. Cover and chill for 10 minutes or until required.

For the salsa, combine all the ingredients in a bowl, season to taste and stir well.

Heat 2.5 cm/1 inch of oil in a wok or deep pan and fry the aubergine balls in batches for 2–3 minutes until golden brown, turning occasionally. Drain on kitchen paper.

Serve the balls in warmed corn tortilla wraps shaped into cones, with the tomato salsa and basil sprigs.

meatball sandwich

serves 4

450 g/1 lb lean minced beef

1 small onion, grated

2 cloves garlic, crushed

25 g/1 oz fine white breadcrumbs

1 tsp hot chilli sauce

salt and pepper

wholemeal flour, for dusting

groundnut oil, for shallow frying

sandwich

1 tbsp olive oil

1 small onion, sliced

4 sub rolls or small baguettes

4 tbsp mayonnaise

55 g/2 oz sliced jalapeños
(from a jar)

2 tbsp squeezy mustard

Place the minced beef, onion, garlic, breadcrumbs and chilli sauce into a bowl. Season to taste and mix thoroughly. Shape the mixture into 20 small equal-sized balls using floured hands. Cover and chill for 10 minutes or until required.

Heat a shallow depth of oil in a wok or heavy frying pan until very hot, then fry the meatballs in batches for 6–8 minutes, turning often, until golden brown and firm. Drain on kitchen paper and keep hot.

To make the sandwich, heat the olive oil in a clean pan and fry the onions on a moderate heat, stirring occasionally, until soft and golden brown.

Split the rolls lengthwise and spread with mayonnaise. Arrange the onions, meatballs and jalapeños over the bottom half, squeeze the mustard over and top with the other half. Serve the rolls immediately.

lamb & olive meatballs

serves 4-6

500 g/1 lb 2 oz lean minced lamb

1 medium onion, finely chopped

1 clove garlic, crushed

2 tbsp chopped mint

salt and pepper

20 pitted black olives

10 sheets filo pastry
(approximately)

olive oil, for brushing

Preheat the oven to 190°C/375°F/Gas Mark 5.

Place the minced lamb, onion, garlic and mint into a bowl. Season to taste and mix thoroughly. Divide the meat mixture into 20 equal pieces and shape around the olives to form small balls, enclosing the olive completely.

Cut the filo pastry to make 60 squares, measuring about 12 cm/ 4½ inches. Brush the pastry squares lightly with oil and stack in threes, putting the squares at angles to make star shapes. Place a meatball on each stack and press together at the top to make a 'moneybag' shape.

Place the parcels on a baking sheet, brush with oil and bake in the preheated oven for about 20 minutes, until golden brown.
Serve hot.

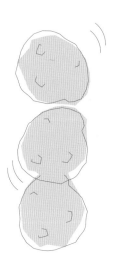

ham & corn meatballs

serves 4

450 g/1 lb lean unsmoked gammon

1 medium onion, quartered

200 g/7 oz can sweetcorn, drained

3 tbsp fine polenta or cornmeal

salt and pepper

groundnut oil, for deep-frying

lemon wedges, to serve

batter

100 g/3½ oz plain flour

1 tsp mild chilli powder

1 egg, beaten

100 ml/3½ fl oz milk and water, mixed

Cut the gammon into chunks, place in a food processor and process for several seconds until finely chopped. Tip into a large bowl.

Finely chop the onion in the food processor and add to the bowl. Roughly process the sweetcorn for a few seconds and add to the bowl. Stir in the polenta, season to taste and mix thoroughly. Shape the mixture into 16 small equal-sized balls. Cover and chill for 10 minutes or until required.

For the batter, place all the ingredients in the food processor and process until smooth and bubbly.

Heat a deep pan of oil to 180°C/350°F or until a cube of bread that is dropped in browns in 30 seconds. Dip each meatball in the batter, drain off the excess and lower into the hot oil. Fry in batches for about 6 minutes each, turning often, until golden brown. Drain on kitchen paper and serve with lemon wedges.

Chilled

chicken & ginger meatballs

serves 4

500 g/1 lb 2 oz skinless, boneless chicken thighs

4 spring onions, roughly chopped

2.5 cm/1 inch piece fresh ginger, grated

15 g/½ oz fresh coriander, roughly chopped

cornflour, for dusting

sesame oil, for greasing

salt and pepper

sweet chilli sauce or soy sauce, to serve

shredded vegetable salad, to serve

Trim any excess fat from the chicken, then place in a food processor with the spring onions, ginger, coriander, salt and pepper. Process in short bursts until very finely chopped but leave some texture.

Shape the mixture into 18–20 small equal-sized balls using floured hands. Cover and chill for 10 minutes or until required.

Pour boiling water into a steamer and bring to the boil. Brush the steamer basket with sesame oil, then add the meatballs. Cover and steam for 12–15 minutes, until firm.

Drain the meatballs, cool completely, then chill before serving. Serve with the sweet chilli sauce for dipping and with a finely shredded vegetable salad.

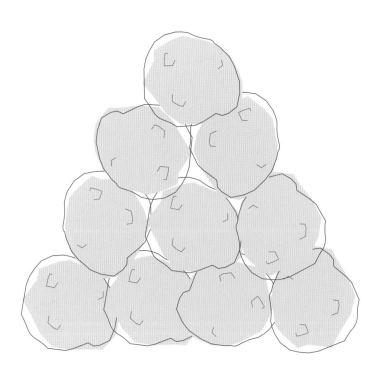

turkey meatballs

serves 4

250 g/9 oz courgettes

3 large shallots, grated

450 g/1 lb minced turkey

55 g/2 oz dry white breadcrumbs

½ tsp grated nutmeg

groundnut oil, for shallow frying

sesame seeds, for coating

salt and pepper

cherry tomatoes and carrot sticks, to serve

Grate the courgettes on a fairly fine grater, or grate in a food processor. Place in a sieve and press out any excess liquid. Place the grated courgette, shallots, turkey, breadcrumbs and nutmeg into a bowl. Season to taste and mix thoroughly. Shape the mixture into 24 small equal-sized balls. Cover and chill for 10 minutes or until required.

Heat 1 cm/½ inch of oil in a wok or heavy frying pan, until a piece of mixture that is dropped in sizzles immediately. Fry the meatballs in batches on a moderate heat for 10–12 minutes, turning often, until golden brown and firm.

Drain the meatballs on kitchen paper, then quickly toss in sesame seeds to coat lightly. Cool completely, then chill and serve cold with cherry tomatoes and carrot sticks.

turkey & spinach meatballs

serves 4

200 g/7 oz cooked young spinach, fresh or frozen

500 g/1 lb 2 oz minced turkey

70 g/2½ oz feta cheese

1 large egg, beaten

85 g/3 oz fresh white breadcrumbs

salt and pepper

groundnut oil, for frying

Place the spinach in a sieve and use a wooden spoon to press out as much moisture as possible. Chop roughly with a sharp knife. Place the spinach and turkey into a bowl. Season to taste and mix thoroughly.

Cut the feta cheese into 16 small chunks. Divide the meat mixture into 16 equal pieces and shape around the feta to form small balls, enclosing the cheese completely. Chill for 10 minutes or until required.

Dip the meatballs in beaten egg to coat lightly, then roll in breadcrumbs to coat evenly.

Heat about a 2.5-cm/1-inch depth of oil in a wok or deep frying pan and fry the meatballs, turning often, for 8–10 minutes or until golden brown and firm. Drain on kitchen paper.

Allow to cool before serving. The meatballs make a good picnic or lunchbox treat.

beef & pecan meatballs

serves 4

500 g/1 lb 2 oz lean minced beef

1 small onion, finely chopped

55 g/2 oz pecan nuts, finely chopped

20 pecan halves

2 tbsp Dijon mustard

2 tbsp maple syrup

1 tbsp olive oil

salt and pepper

Little Gem lettuce leaves, to serve

Preheat the oven to 200°C/400°F/Gas Mark 6.

Place the minced beef, onion and pecans into a bowl. Season to taste and mix thoroughly. Shape the mixture into 20 small equal-sized balls, pressing a pecan half into the top of each. Place on a baking sheet.

Mix together the mustard, maple syrup and oil and brush over the meatballs. Bake in the oven for about 15 minutes, until golden brown and firm.

Cool before serving in the lettuce leaves, placing each on a small leaf to serve as a canapé, or serve in groups on larger leaves for a starter.

pork meatballs

serves 4

groundnut oil, for greasing

500 g/1 lb 2 oz minced pork

1 medium onion, grated

150 g/5½ oz ready-to-eat dried
apricots, finely chopped

1 tbsp Worcestershire sauce

salt and pepper

1 small egg, beaten

100 g/3½ oz pine kernels

Preheat the oven to 180°C/350°F/Gas Mark 4. Lightly grease a
baking sheet.

Place the minced pork, onion, apricots and Worcestershire sauce
into a bowl. Season to taste and mix thoroughly. Shape the mixture
into 24 small equal-sized balls.

Dip the meatballs quickly into the beaten egg then press into the
pine nuts to coat the tops of the meatballs. Place on the prepared
baking sheet.

Bake the meatballs in the preheated oven for about 15 minutes,
until firm and golden brown. Cool completely, then chill
until required.

salmon sushi balls

serves 6-8

400 g/14 oz sushi rice

600 ml/1 pint water

2 tbsp rice vinegar

2 tsp caster sugar

1 tsp salt

2 tsp grated fresh ginger

150 g/5½ oz sliced smoked salmon

sprigs of fresh dill to garnish

wasabi to serve

Wash the rice thoroughly under running cold water and drain.

Place the rice in a heavy-based pan with the water, cover and bring to the boil. Leave to simmer on a moderate heat for 10 minutes. Reduce the heat to very low and leave for a further 5 minutes. Remove from the heat and leave to cool, still covered.

Place the vinegar, sugar, salt, ginger and rice into a bowl. Mix thoroughly. Shape the mixture into 30 small equal-sized balls.

Cut the salmon into 3–4 cm/1¾–1½-inch squares. Place a sprig of dill onto a 15-cm/6-inch square of clingfilm, top with a square of salmon and a rice ball, gather up the edges of the clingfilm and twist to make a firm ball. Repeat to make about 30 wraps and chill in the refrigerator for at least 20 minutes.

Unwrap the rice balls and serve cold as a canapé or starter, with a dab of wasabi on the side.

crabmeat balls

serves 4

85 g/3 oz matzo crackers or cream crackers, finely crushed

200 g/7 oz dressed crabmeat (white and dark)

1 egg white

4 spring onions, very finely chopped

1 small red chilli, deseeded and finely chopped

juice of ½ lime

Preheat the oven to 220°C/425°F/Gas Mark 7.

Reserve 15 g/½ oz of the cracker crumbs. Place the remaining crackers, crabmeat, egg white, onions, chilli and lime juice into a bowl. Mix thoroughly, adding extra lime juice if necessary. Shape the mixture into 16 equal-sized balls.

Roll in the reserved cracker crumbs to coat lightly and arrange on a baking sheet.

Bake the crabmeat balls in the preheated oven for about 10 minutes, until lightly browned and crisp. Cool before serving as a canapé, or with salad leaves for a starter.

mushroom & bean balls

serves 4-6

350 g/12 oz cup mushrooms,
quartered

1 small onion, quartered

420 g/15 oz can red kidney beans,
drained thoroughly

1 clove garlic, crushed

1 tbsp chopped thyme

1 small egg, beaten

85 g/3 oz fresh wholemeal
breadcrumbs

salt and pepper

wholemeal flour, for dusting

groundnut oil, for shallow frying

avocado dip

1 ripe avocado

juice of 1 small lemon

1 tsp chopped thyme

salt and pepper

Place the mushrooms and onion in a food processor and process until finely chopped. Add the beans, garlic, thyme, egg and breadcrumbs and process in short bursts until the mixture just binds together. Season with salt and pepper.

Shape the mixture into 20 equal-sized balls using lightly floured hands. Heat 1-cm/½-inch depth of oil in a wok or heavy frying pan and fry the balls, turning often, until golden brown. Drain on kitchen paper. Cool.

For the dip, purée the avocado flesh with the lemon juice and thyme, season to taste and serve with the mushroom balls.